The Nature Kid's Guide to

OCELOTS

DAVID ANDERSON

LP Media Inc. Publishing
Text copyright © 2026 by LP Media Inc.

For information address LP Media Inc. Publishing,
30012 Variolite St NW, Princeton MN 55371
www.lpmedia.org

Publication Data

Ocelots
The Nature Kid's Guide to Ocelots — First edition.

Summary: "Learn all about Ocelots, the Nature Kid Way"
— Provided by publisher.

ISBN: 979-8-89818-256-4

[1. Ocelots – Non-Fiction] I. Title.

Title: The Nature Kid's Guide to Ocelots

CONTENTS

JUNGLE JEWELS

Ocelots are super **adaptable!** They can live on sandy beaches, in steamy jungles, or high up on misty mountains.

Rustle! An ocelot slinks through the thick, green jungle.

Ocelots are wild cats that live in warm, green forests. They love thick plants and shady trees. The jungle is their perfect home!

Big leaves and tall vines give ocelots good cover. Thick plants grow close together on the forest floor, keeping the air cool and damp. An ocelot can vanish into this green world in seconds.

The forest gives them all they need. It has food, water, and cozy spots to sleep. What a great place to be an ocelot!

WILD HOMES

Fewer than 100 ocelots still live wild in the United States. Thousands once roamed Texas, Louisiana, Arkansas, and Arizona.

Whoosh! An ocelot dashes across a moonlit forest path.

Ocelots live in many lands. You can find them in Mexico and Central America. They also roam across most of South America.

A few ocelots even live in the United States! A small group calls southern Texas home. That is the only U.S. spot where they live in the wild.

From Brazil to Texas, these cats roam far and wide. But they always pick warm lands with lots of plant cover to hide in.

SMALL SPOTS

FUN FACT!
The ocelot is the third-largest wild cat in the Americas, after the jaguar and puma!

Thump! A spotted ocelot jumps from a tree and lands softly on the ground below.

A full grown ocelot is roughly twice the size of a house cat, but built lean and low to the ground. That compact shape is perfectly designed for life in dense jungle.

Most ocelots weigh between 20 and 35 pounds — about as heavy as a small dog. Add a foot-long ringed tail to their three-foot body and they are a surprisingly long cat for their weight.

Even though they are small, ocelots are strong and **agile**. Their slim build lets them slip through tangled brush without slowing down.

SPOTTED STYLE

Ocelot kittens are born with bright blue eyes that slowly change to golden brown by the time they are three months old!

Patter! An ocelot trots from the shade, its golden fur shining.

Ocelots have golden or tan fur covered with dark spots and stripes. Each ocelot has its own pattern, like a fingerprint. No two look exactly alike!

Their fur is short and smooth. Black lines run along their cheeks and neck, while white fur marks their belly and chin.

Ocelots also have round ears with a white spot on the back. Their short tails have dark rings near the tip. Every part of their coat helps them blend into the forest shadows.

SUPER SENSES

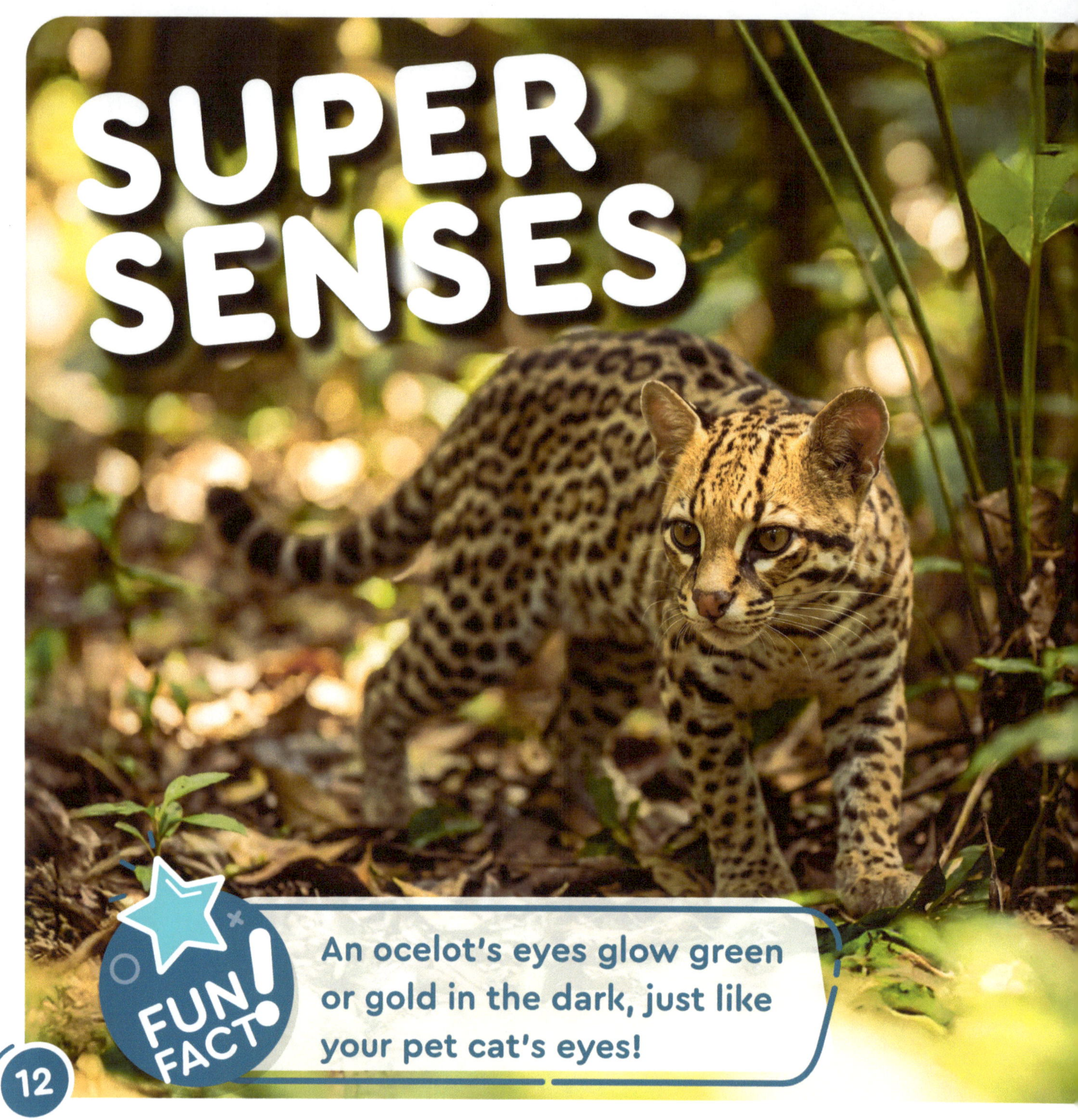

Squeak! An ocelot hears a tiny mouse creep through the leaves.

Ocelots have some of the best senses in the cat world. Their big eyes take in lots of light, helping them see well at night. They can spot a mouse moving 50 feet away in near darkness!

Their ears turn and twist to catch every sound. Even a tiny step in the grass gets noticed. Ocelots can hear prey from far away.

Long whiskers help them feel their way through the dark. Their strong nose picks up smells that lead them straight to food.

SNEAKY SPOTS

Shh! Can you spot the ocelot hiding in the leafy shade?

An ocelot's spots are not just pretty. They help it hide! The dark marks break up its shape in the shadows.

When light shines through the trees, it makes patches on the ground. The ocelot's coat looks just like those patches. This trick is called camouflage.

Staying hidden keeps ocelots safe from danger. They blend into the forest so well that even sharp eyes can miss them. A still ocelot is almost invisible.

MEATY MENU

Yum! An ocelot swallows a bite of meat from its fresh catch.

Ocelots eat meat. They hunt small animals like mice, rats, and rabbits. Birds, lizards, and frogs are also on the menu.

These cats sometimes catch fish from streams. They also eat crabs, snakes, and even small monkeys. Ocelots are not picky eaters at all!

An ocelot eats its catch right away and does not save food for later. Each night brings a new hunt and a fresh meal.

An ocelot can gobble up three pounds of meat in one night. That is like eating 12 hamburgers!

POUNCE POWER

Jump! An ocelot pounces and pins down a small rodent.

Ocelots are great hunters. They walk slowly and quietly through the forest. When they spot prey, they freeze and wait.

Then they pounce! An ocelot leaps and grabs its prey in a flash. The attack is so fast that the prey cannot escape.

Ocelots also sniff the ground to find trails left by other animals. They follow these paths with care. Hunting takes lots of skill and patience.

Ocelots pluck off every single feather from a bird before eating it. They are very tidy hunters!

BIG BULLIES

DID YOU KNOW?
A full-grown jaguar can weigh 150 pounds or more. That is about five times heavier than an ocelot!

Growl! A jaguar prowls near, and the ocelot stays still.

Even the best hunter can be hunted. Jaguars and pumas will attack ocelots. These big cats are much stronger and faster.

Large eagles can swoop down and grab an ocelot. Big snakes like boas can also be a danger. Even wild dogs may go after a young ocelot.

Young ocelots face the most risk because they are small and cannot fight back. For them, staying hidden is the best way to stay safe.

QUICK ESCAPE

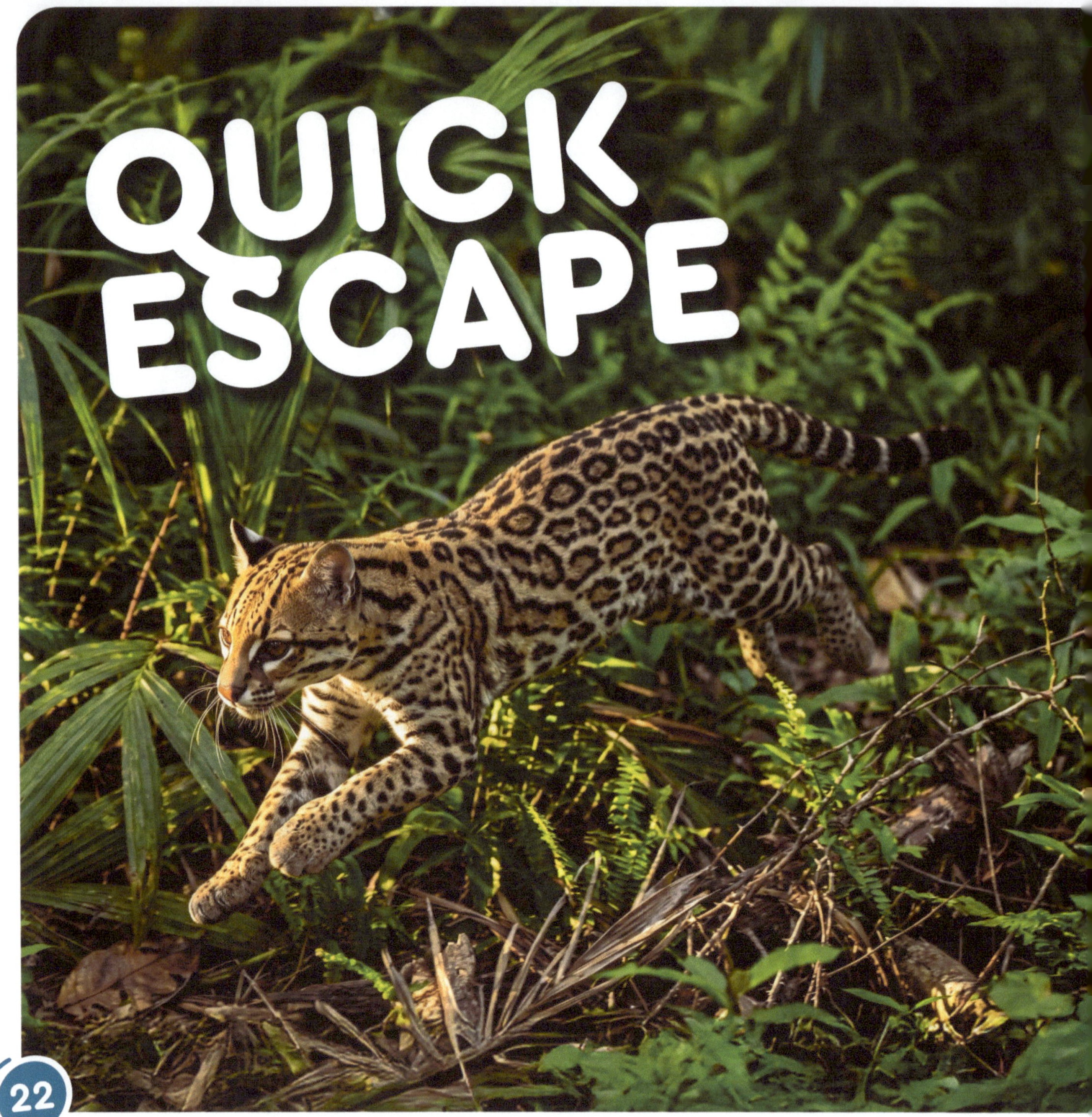

Zoom! An ocelot races through the brush to escape danger.

When danger is near, ocelots know what to do. They can run very fast to get away, and their quick legs carry them through thick brush.

Ocelots also leap up into trees when scared. A tall tree keeps them safe from a hungry jaguar. They can wait up high until the danger passes.

Sometimes running will not work. Then an ocelot hides in a hole or **den**. It will use every trick it knows to survive.

An ocelot can spin and change direction in mid-run. This zigzag move confuses bigger predators!

CLIMB HIGH

An ocelot's back legs are longer than its front legs. This gives them extra power for jumping and climbing!

Scratch! An ocelot digs its claws into bark and climbs up.

Ocelots love to climb. Their sharp claws grip bark as they go up, and they can reach high into the treetops with ease.

These cats are good swimmers too. They cross streams and rivers to find food or explore new areas. Water does not scare them one bit.

On the ground, ocelots walk softly on padded paws. They can sneak through the forest without making a sound. Every step is smooth, quiet, and careful.

NIGHT NINJA

DID YOU KNOW?
One ocelot may walk more than five miles in a single night. That is like walking across 88 football fields!

Hoot! The owl calls, and the ocelot begins its nightly hunt.

Ocelots are most active at night. When the sun goes down, they wake up and start moving. The dark forest is their playground.

During the day, ocelots sleep in hidden spots. They curl up in hollow trees or rocky dens, resting for up to 12 hours. A long nap gets them ready for the busy night ahead.

As the stars come out, the ocelot goes to work. It walks for miles, looking for food. The night is the best time to find a tasty meal.

SOLO STALKERS

If two male ocelots meet, they may growl, hiss, and fight over space. These battles can get fierce!

Hiss! Two ocelots meet at the border of their forest areas.

Ocelots like to live alone. Each one claims its own area of forest and does not share space with other ocelots.

An ocelot marks its area with **scent**. It rubs on trees and sprays to leave its smell behind. This warns other ocelots to stay out.

Male ocelots claim bigger areas than females. A male's space may overlap with areas used by a few females. But two males will not share the same land without a fight.

LOVE CALLS

Ocelots can meow, growl, hiss, and even purr, just like your pet cat at home!

Yowl! A loud cry fills the forest as an ocelot calls for a mate.

When it is time to find a mate, ocelots get noisy. Males make loud, long calls in the night. Females call back to say where they are.

Once they meet, a male and female may spend a few days together. They rub heads, lick each other, and stay close. After that, the male goes back to living alone.

Ocelots can have babies at any time of year. There is no special season for new kittens to arrive!

CUTE KITTENS

Mew! A tiny ocelot kitten opens its eyes for the first time.

Baby ocelots are called kittens. A mother usually has one or two kittens at a time, and they are born in a safe, hidden den.

Newborn kittens are tiny. They weigh less than one pound! Their eyes stay closed for about two weeks after birth.

The kittens have soft, fuzzy fur with faint spots. Even as babies, they start to look like little wild cats. They grow fast on their mother's rich milk.

MOM MATTERS

The father ocelot never helps raise the kittens. Mom does all the work by herself!

Purr! A mother ocelot licks her kitten clean after a meal.

Mother ocelots take good care of their kittens. They keep the den clean and safe. If danger is near, a mother moves her babies fast.

As kittens grow, the mother brings them bits of meat. She teaches them how to **stalk** and catch prey. These hunting lessons start when they are just a few months old.

Young ocelots stay with their mother for up to two years. After that, they leave to find a home of their own and begin life as solo hunters.

LOSING HOMES

Crash! Trees fall as machines clear land where ocelots live.

Ocelots are in trouble. People cut down forests to build roads and farms. When trees are gone, ocelots lose their homes.

Long ago, people hunted ocelots for their fur. They made coats and bags from the spotted skins. This killed many, many ocelots.

Today, cars are also a big danger. Ocelots cross busy roads at night and can be hit. Lost forests and fast cars both make life hard for these beautiful cats.

SAVING OCELOTS

Thanks to new laws and protected lands, ocelot numbers are slowly starting to grow again!

Click! A camera trap takes a photo of a wild ocelot at night.

Ocelots are getting help from people all over the world. Laws now keep them safe from hunters, and no one can sell ocelot fur anymore.

Groups plant trees and protect forests where ocelots live. They also build safe paths under roads. These wildlife crossings help ocelots travel without getting hit by cars.

Scientists use cameras in the wild to track ocelots. Every photo helps them learn more about these shy cats. With help, ocelots can have a bright future ahead.

GLOSSARY

den

A safe, hidden place where an animal rests

stalk

To follow slowly and quietly before attacking

scent

A smell left behind by an animal

adaptable

Able to survive and thrive in many different places and conditions

agile

Able to move quickly and easily with great balance and speed